[illegible] TONIGHT

I tra [illegible] pre-biblical times. Perhaps all this research affected my personal life, as I practised not having sex through three marriages and four divorces. I certainly enjoyed not having sex with them all, and we're still good friends. I do not regret any sacrifice I have made to further the cause of not having sex tonight. In an attempt to make rhyme or reason out of the whole bloody business, I have spent many tedious years interviewing men and women to find out their reasons for not having sex tonight, tomorrow morning, or tomorrow afternoon.

From the thousands of reasons put to me, I have sifted out 101 of the best. If you have a better one, send it to me. I'll use it.

Get out of bed and live!

Dr Potent trained in Vienna before discovering the joy of not having sex. He is now widely recognised as the world's leading non-sexologist.

Other books by I. M. Potent, M.D.

Don't Show Me
How to Lose Weight While Not Having Sex
It's Not Your Body
Keep Your Shirt On!
Your Endzones; How to Avoid Them

101 REASONS NOT TO HAVE SEX TONIGHT

I. M. Potent, M.D.
Illustrated by Comfort and Joy

Star
A STAR BOOK
published by
the Paperback Division of
W. H. ALLEN & Co. Ltd

A Star Book
Published in 1981
by the Paperback Division of
W. H. Allen & Co. Ltd
A Howard and Wyndham Company
44 Hill Street, London W1X 8LB

First published in the United States by
Harmony Books, 1981

Printed in Great Britain by The Anchor Press Ltd, Tiptree, Essex

ISBN 0 352 30923 7

*To Maria, who taught me so much
about not having sex tonight*

Men (and women too) spend less time having sex tonight than the average insect.

B. P. Defarges, noted naturalist

CONTENTS

THE POTENT PHILO-SOPHY

The young Potent. Even at this age he showed a great interest in not having sex.

GET OUT OF BED AND LIVE!

I have often been asked when and how I became interested in not having sex, and frankly I don't know the answer to that one. I think I was always interested in not having sex. Of course, it runs in the family. My mother and dad, Emma Grassfarber and E. S. Potent, enjoyed not having sex in a rowboat during their courtship and on their honeymoon. How I was born is a mystery to me—a mystery I am currently delving into.

I was rejected by young girls in the neighborhood as well as by my maiden aunt with the mustache. My mother and my grandfather also spurned my advances. In fact, my mother slapped my face and told me not having sex was a dirty thing. (I hadn't realized it until then.) My great-uncle, A. A. Potent, famous for his striking resemblance to Sigmund Freud, greatly influenced me in my desire to know more about not having sex tonight—or

A rare photograph of Dr I. M. Potent's mother on her wedding night.

Dr I. M. Potent's father in his prime. He was famous for not having sex in the house.

tomorrow morning for that matter. Could the study of not having sex be an exact science? Who knows? But I was determined to push on and find out. I studied girlie magazines of the thirties *(Film Fun, Spicy Detective)* and worked my way up (if you'll pardon the expression) to *Playboy, Penthouse,* and *Hustler.* I found them disgusting and they hardened my resolve (if you'll pardon the expression) to spread the word. *Don't have sex tonight!*

I traced the history of not having sex back to pre-biblical times (would you believe it). Something that old just has to be good. I also made an extensive study of not having sex in the animal kingdom. And the things I found out about chickens. Well, believe you me, that could fill another book! Perhaps all this research affected my personal life, as I practiced not having sex through three marriages and four divorces. I certainly enjoyed not having sex with them all, and we're still good friends. In the course of my studies I discovered the non-erogenous zones (or bones) of the body. My work in this area has yet to be recognized by the AMA.

But back to business. I do not regret any sacrifice I have made to further the cause of not having sex tonight. In an attempt to make rhyme or reason out of the whole bloody business, I have spent many tedious years interviewing men and women to find out their reasons for not having sex tonight, tomorrow morning, or tomorrow afternoon.

From the thousands of reasons put to me, I have sifted out 101 of the best.

If a reason fits, use it.

If you have a better one, send it to me. I'll use it.

Get out of bed and live!

THE POTENT REPORT: SECTION ONE

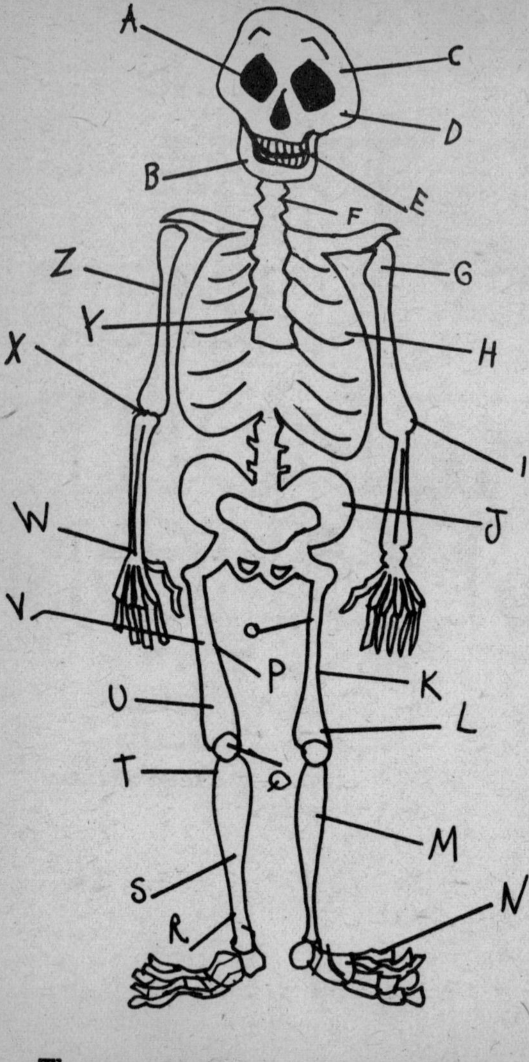

The non-erogenous zones of the body.

101 REASONS **NOT** TO HAVE SEX TONIGHT

and The Gallery of Non-Erotic Art

1. I have a headache.

2. It's caught in the mousetrap.

3. We did it *last* month.

4. I've got to talk to the plants.

5. If I'm not there in fifteen minutes, start without me.

6. You didn't tell me you had false teeth.

7. I can't get my boots off.

8. I can't get my boots on.

Sarcophagus, the founder of the not having sex tonight movement.

9. The parakeet is watching.

10. I'm with the vice squad and you're under arrest!

11. *The Night of the Living Dead* is on TV.

12. You'll smear my mudpack.

13. Check it out with my lawyer.

Dear Dr. Potent:

My boyfriend and I enjoy not having sex wearing diapers and talking baby talk to each other. Are we okay?

Babyface and Snookums

Dear Babyface and Snookums:

You're adorable! And you're okay too.

I.M.P.

14. I'm going home to Mother.

15. The hand brake is in the way.

16. I had a sex change operation yesterday.

17. The bed's broken.

18. The burglar alarm just went off!

19. You rub me the wrong way.

20. Granny's peeking.

Greek vase illustrating positions not to have sex for humans, animals, and insects.

Rare print by Karasa Mishegaas illustrating the tree position.

Dear Dr. Potent:

I derive incredible pleasure from watching people not having sex. Am I a voyeur?

Tom

Dear Tom:

Yes.

I.M.P.

21. There's always next year.

22. Twelve times is enough.

23. It's Yom Kippur.

24. I prefer lollipops.

25. I think sex is dirty.

26. Thanks for not smoking.

27. I've got my mother on hold.

28. The water bed is leaking.

29. Not without my teddy bear.

30. I can't rise to the occasion.

Early Eskimo drawing illustrating the nose-to-nose position.

31. I already gave at the office.

32. Why spoil a perfect friendship?

33. I just brushed my teeth.

34. I forgot my flippers.

35. It's the anniversary of my gerbil's death.

Indian separate bottle position.

36. I have to finish *War and Peace* first.

37. I can't do it without Jell-O.

38. I lent *The Joy of Sex* to my dad.

39. I get dizzy upside down.

Dear Dr. Potent:

I'm a traveling salesman. I came home from work early yesterday and found my wife not having sex with my best friend. What should I do?

Willie

Dear Willie:

Does your wife have a best friend?

I.M.P.

40. I refuse to lend you my garter belt.

41. I've donated my body to science.

42. I lost the instructions.

43. I'm dying for a corned beef sandwich.

44. Mirrors make me reflective.

45. We're out of Kleenex.

46. I just took a bottle of sleeping pills.

Early Japanese print illustrating the how not to have sex in a swing position.

Unsigned sketch by unknown modern artist depicting a young girl not having sex with herself.

Dear Dr. Potent:

I am a lieutenant in the Navy, and while on tour I did not have sex with the entire crew of a submarine. Should I tell my wife?

Confused

Dear Confused:

Don't. She'd probably torpedo you.

I.M.P.

47. My heart belongs to Daddy.

48. After my nap.

49. I can't find the whip and chains.

50. Only handcuffs?

51. The bathtub is overflowing.

52. I'm ticklish.

53. We're out of whipped cream.

54. I always sleep in my panty hose.

55. The bed is bugged.

56. I've just had oral surgery.

Minotaur pursuing maiden (motive unclear).

57. What about the neighbors?

58. We can't make ends meet.

59. I swallowed my pacifier.

60. The trapeze is broken.

Dear Dr. Potent:

My husband insists on not having sex with me three or four times a week. I am exhausted. What should I do?

Frazzled

Dear Frazzled:

If you're exhausted now, just thank your lucky stars that he doesn't come home at lunchtime.

I.M.P.

61. You don't send me flowers anymore.

62. I'm waiting for the tooth fairy.

63. The batteries are dead.

64. Z-Z-Z-Z-Z.

65. I have to make an obscene phone call.

66. Can't we just be roommates?

67. The Polaroid's jammed.

68. I just had a shower and I don't want to get all sweaty.

69. My boyfriend wouldn't like it.

70. My girl friend wouldn't like it.

71. Your mustache tickles.

Easter Island statues illustrating the look-no-hands position. That is Dr. Potent in the pith helmet.

72. My nail polish is still wet.

73. I didn't have enough to drink.

74. The sofa bed is stuck.

75. *Heeeeere's Johnnyyy!!!!*

Dear Dr. Potent:

Is obesity a hindrance to not having sex? I weigh 330 pounds.

Tubby

Dear Tubby:

Your obesity will be a great asset to you in not having sex. Don't lose weight!

I.M.P.

76. NO!

77. I can't light your fire without a blow-torch.

78. The cat feels left out.

79. I don't *need* to lose any more weight.

Dear Dr. Potent:

I am a twenty-two-year-old bisexual divorcée with a young son. My problem is that I enjoy not having sex with both sexes. Can you help me?

Pearl

Dear Pearl:

Can you help me?

I.M.P.

Rare Persian print illustrating the toe-to-toe position.

Dear Dr. Potent:

My husband broke his false teeth and lost his contact lenses while not having sex with me last night. What should I do?

Helpless and Hopeless in SoHo

Dear Helpless and Hopeless in SoHo:

Not having sex can be dangerous and exciting. You and your husband prove it.

I.M.P.

80. Not in the *nude!*

81. I don't feel like it tonight, Sam, I mean Murray.

82. I'm a virgin!

83. The honeymoon is *over.*

84. You didn't even pick up the check.

85. I lost my contact lens.

86. I've got the hic-hic-hiccups.

87. I've got a sink full of dirty dishes.

88. I'm worn out from the candlelight dinner.

89. I can't find the microscope.

90. Do you have an appointment?

91. It doesn't come with the blue plate special.

92. I hardly know where to begin.

93. It's illegal, immoral, and fattening.

94. I'm not insured.

95. My license has expired.

96. I don't accept checks.

97. It's not Thursday.

98. I get off at the next stop.

Maiden hurrying to secret place not to have sex. Artist unknown.

99. You remind me of Mother.

100. You *must* be kidding.

101. Let's not and *say* we did!

THE BEST **POSITIONS** FOR NOT HAVING SEX

POSITION #1

Ménage à Trois: One Female, Two Males

These positions are illustrated with line drawings rather than photographs with the hope they will in no way incite lust.

POSITION #2

Kneeling
Face to Face

If you have housemaid's knee, avoid this position.

POSITION #3

TV Position

Restful and soothing after a trying day. One or both partners often doze off.

POSITION #4

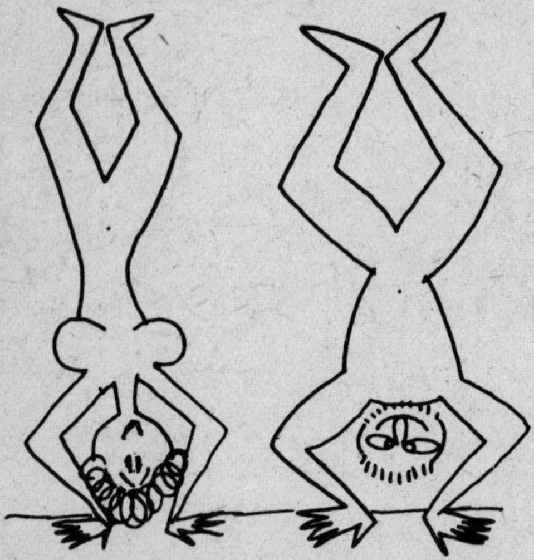

The Double Headstand

This position has replaced the double standard, but not the double bed.

POSITION #5

Roller Disco Position

Only if your partner is a good skate.

POSITION #6

Seated with Table Between, and Hands on Table

A variation of this position is putting food on the table. Many couples do this three times a day.

POSITION #7

Hanging from the Chandelier

Light up your life with this swinging position.

POSITION #8

Non-Oral Position

Much favored by dentists and root canal specialists.

POSITION #9

Teeter-Totter or Seesaw Position

Brings you back to happy childhood days but has its ups and downs.

POSITION #10

Male Standing on Hands, Female Standing on Feet

This position puts quite a strain on the male and should not be attempted without consulting your physician or visiting nurse.

POSITION #11

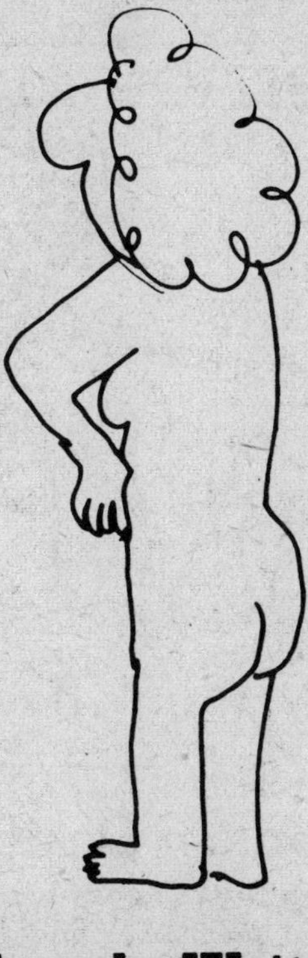

Female Waiting, Male Working Late at Office

Not entirely effective if male has a young secretary.

POSITION #12

Missionary Position

For those with a religious bent. This position has many converts.

POSITION #13

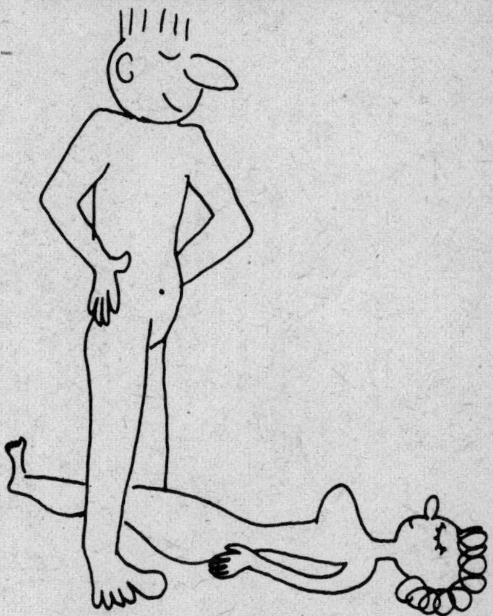

Male Superior

You don't see much of this position these days.

POSITION #14

Ménage à Trois: One Male, Two Females

This is a lot of fun and is also known as the double date.

POSITION #15

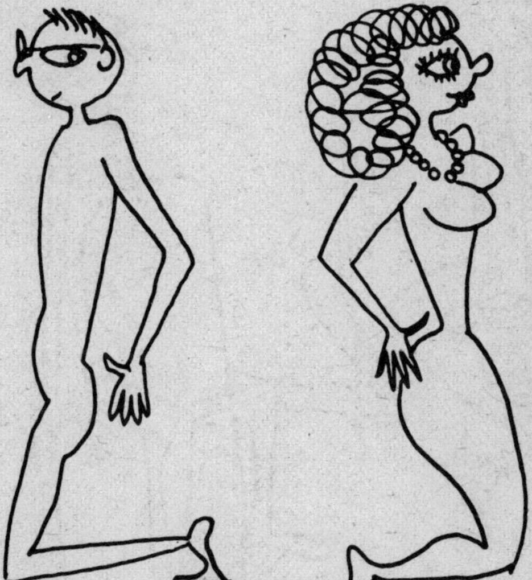

Kneeling
Back to Back

Gives the minimum body and eye contact. Recommended for the very shy.

POSITION #16

Reverse Chair Position Face to Face

For added fun, try rocking chairs.

POSITION #17

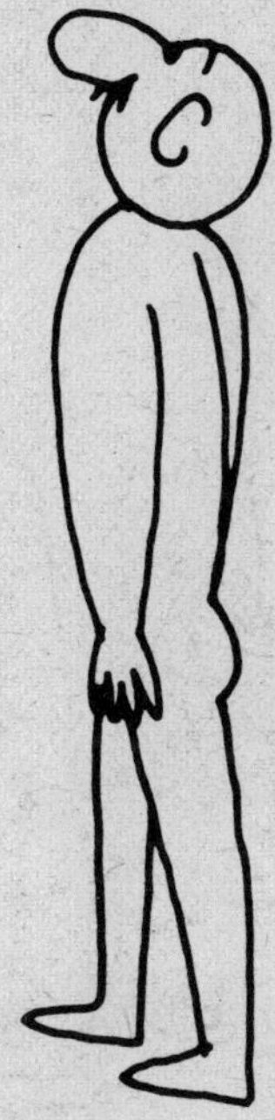

Male Standing, Female Out Shopping

A familiar sight in the suburbs as well as in urban shopping centers.

POSITION #18

Female Kneeling on Floor, Male Kneeling on Female's Head and

POSITION #19

Male Kneeling on Floor, Female Kneeling on Male's Head

Favored by hardheaded people of both sexes.

POSITION #20

Froggy Position

Don't try it if you think you'll croak.

POSITION #21

Doggy Position

Bone up on this one.

POSITION #22

Telephone Booth Position

The cramped quarters create a special intimacy. Nice if you want to call home.

POSITION #23

Rubber Ducky Position

Make sure you have enough ducks. Six are recommended.

POSITION #24

The Drinky-Poo Position

Fully clothed—dangerous if unclothed.

THE BEST **PLACES** NOT TO HAVE SEX

1. Times Square on New Year's Eve
2. The White House lawn on Easter Sunday
3. Under the clock at the Biltmore
4. Snow White's cottage at Disneyland
5. Fisherman's Wharf when the fleet comes in
6. Central Park after dark
7. Red Square on May Day
8. Macy's windows
9. The center ring at the circus
10. Mount Everest in January

THE BEST **MOVIES** TO WATCH WHILE NOT HAVING SEX

1. *Nanook of the North*

2. *Snow White*

3. *Les Miserables*

4. *The Ten Commandments*

5. *Close Encounters of the Third Kind*

6. *Repulsion*

7. *The Sound of Music*

8. *Invasion of the Body Snatchers*

9. *Gidget Goes Hawaiian*

10. Any Ronald Reagan picture

THE BEST **FOODS** TO EAT BEFORE NOT HAVING SEX

1. Beans
2. Prunes
3. Banana cream pie
4. Breast of chicken
5. Coq au vin
6. Beans
7. Tongue sandwich on whole-wheat toast
8. French bread
9. Greek salad
10. Beans

THE BEST **BEVERAGES** TO DRINK WHILE NOT HAVING SEX

1. Warm milk

2. Perrier water

3. Root-beer float

4. V-8 juice

5. Alka-Seltzer

6. Dr. Pepper

7. Ovaltine

8. Any diet soda

9. Cranberry juice

10. Ice water

THE BEST **MUSIC** TO LISTEN TO WHILE NOT HAVING SEX

1. "The Stars and Stripes Forever!"
2. "Satisfaction"
3. *Naughty Marietta*
4. Ravel's "Bolero"
5. "When the Saints Go Marching In"
6. "Rock-a-Bye Baby"
7. "When I Grow Too Old to Dream"
8. "Silver Threads Among the Gold"
9. "Drink to Me Only with Thine Eyes"
10. "I Wanna Hold Your Hand"

THE BEST **CLOTHES** TO WEAR WHILE NOT HAVING SEX

1. Heavy tweeds
2. Rubber boots
3. Bulletproof vest
4. Crinoline
5. Rubber diving suit and mask
6. Spurs
7. Golf socks
8. Uniform of the Coldstream Guards
9. Puttees
10. Gorilla suit

THE BEST **COSTUMES** TO WEAR WHILE NOT HAVING SEX

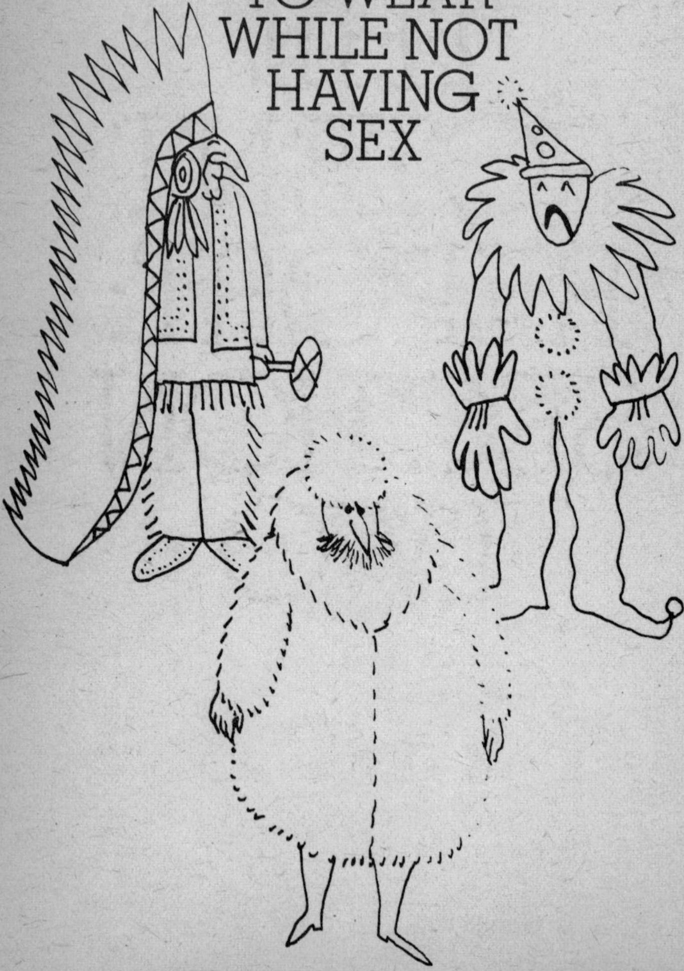

THE POTENT REPORT: SECTION TWO

NOT HAVING SEX THROUGH THE AGES: AN ORAL HISTORY

Not having sex tonight was invented by the ancient Egyptians. Their non-mating call was TUT TUT.

Not having sex tonight was not very popular in biblical times, although the practice enjoyed a slight revival after Sodom and Gomorrah.

The ancient Romans held large group meetings where the participants enjoyed not having sex with one another. These meetings were called norgies.

Some scholars take the position that the Greeks invented not having sex tonight but restricted its practice to men and/or chubby boys.

The Crusaders took it with them to the Holy Land where it soon became popular, not to mention wide-spread.

Not having sex was quite the rage in England

during the Age of Chivalry, as the suits of armor worn by the Knights of the Round Table were the perfect garment for not having sex in. Camelot was a veritable cesspool.

The Dark Ages drove the delicate practice underground, and having sex became very popular, especially on rainy afternoons. This brought disease and pestilence, not to mention rats.

Fortunately, the Renaissance brought a revival of not having sex, particularly among the upper classes. Among the more well known practitioners was Dante, who did not have sex with Beatrice, among others. The Borgias practiced not having sex, as did Michelangelo who, although he spent a lot of time on his back, was not in that position for the usual reasons.

When Columbus discovered America, he introduced the gentle science to the natives, who started scalping people shortly thereafter.

There is some doubt whether the witches of Salem did or didn't. Only the inquisitors knew for sure.

As America moved westward, not having sex tonight helped pass many a lonely night in the covered wagon.

There was a flowering of not having sex tonight during Victorian times. The practice was secretly espoused by Queen Victoria herself as well as Prince Albert, who later had a pipe tobacco named after him.

Today, there are more converts than ever to the ancient art. Always remember, dear friends, having sex has caused more marriages and divorces than I care to mention. Don't have sex with someone you love tonight; you might enjoy it.

NOT HAVING SEX IN THE ANIMAL KINGDOM

The dinosaurs were the first practitioners of not having sex in the animal kingdom. Contrary to popular belief, the birds and the bees spend more time not having sex than the reverse. The same holds true for rabbits. Giraffes definitely do not have sex (how could they?), but they do a lot of (you'll pardon the expression) necking. Worms, when they're not fishing, do not have sex with themselves as they can't find anybody else not to have sex with. Salmon are known to swim upstream not to have sex with another salmon, and I consider that pretty romantic, don't you? And they call them cold fish.

I won't even get into whales not having sex, or penguins, or that most intelligent of creatures, the dolphin. I have spent many happy and fruitless hours watching dolphins disporting and not having sex with one another, and then discussing it with them. Chickens have always been an enigma to me. You know the trumpet call of the elephant. He's calling another elephant (of the opposite sex, I presume) so they cannot have sex together. No wonder the ivory hunters are gnashing their teeth. Well, nuts to them.

It is sunset. Crawl silently with me through the jungle underbrush (be careful of the poison ivy) as we view the kings and queens of the jungle drinking deep at their favorite wateringhole before finding a partner to spend the night not having sex with. Oh, no. There's a naughty tsetse fly. Bad fly, don't look at him!

THE "LET'S NOT HAVE SEX TONIGHT" HOROSCOPE

What does the future hold in store for you? Will you not be having sex tonight with a mysterious stranger? Gaze at the stars with me and find out.

ARIES
March 21–April 19

You've heard the phrase Airie-Fairie? Well, look out. You need a lot of petting and pampering but don't go all the way. Not having sex with a stranger has its allure, but be faithful. If you can't be faithful, be careful.

TAURUS
April 20–May 20

You're great at shooting the bull. You are easily tempted, but avoid temptation. Do not have sex with anybody for the rest of the year. Do you hear me? Well, don't say I didn't warn you.

GEMINI

May 21–June 21

Double trouble. You enjoy not having sex with twins, and I can't say that I blame you. When your ego is low, it's hard to get a rise out of you. You are a real pain in the behind, and it's a mystery to me why anyone would want to have sex with you.

CANCER

June 22–July 22

You are a clinger. The way to your stomach is through your heart. The way to your liver is through your gallbladder. The way to your spleen is through your unmentionables. The way to the bathroom is straight back, then turn left, knock three times and ask for José. I definitely do *not* want to have sex with you.

LEO

July 23–August 22

You are romantic and vulnerable. I think it's about time you grew up. When did you start not having sex? Where is the first person you did not have sex with? (Male or female as the case may be.) Oh, how easily you Leos forget.

VIRGO

August 23–September 22

Well, you know what Virgo stands for and I hope you still are. Stay as sweet as you are—get interested in winter sports, summer sports, anything. You have a brain—use it. Keep your body under wraps. Bottoms up!

LIBRA
September 23–October 23

You are in love with not having sex in the morning, afternoon, and evening, not to mention midnight snacks. Keep a tight rein on yourself. Don't make any financial commitments in August; stay loose and stop trying to make (excuse me) ends meet.

SCORPIO
October 24–November 21

You are not very sexy. Not having sex comes easily to you. You attract other people who are not interested in having sex. You are kind, considerate, and helpful.

SAGITTARIUS
November 22–December 21

You like not having sex outdoors, in trees, on picnic tables, and under the stars. Try someplace unusual, like a bed. This could put new vitality into your nonsex life. Try not touching.

CAPRICORN
December 22–January 19

You enjoy not having sex under the Christmas tree. You secretly yearn for Santa Claus (or Mrs. Claus as the case may be). You fill your Christmas stocking well. Merry Christmas and a Happy New Year.

AQUARIUS
January 20–February 18

You will not be having sex tonight with a tall dark stranger if you're female or with a short dumpy blonde if you're a male. If you swing both ways, good. Send a present to someone you don't want to have sex with and avoid sudden career decisions. If you are male, you are intrigued with the idea of becoming a male stripper.

PISCES

February 19–March 20

Something fishy here. You are a dreamer and I hate to tell you what you are dreaming about. You hit a low before you hit a high. Your self-confidence needs building up. Not having sex might be the answer.

MYTHS AND MISCONCEPTIONS ABOUT NOT HAVING SEX

1. You can get pregnant by not having sex tonight. (False.)

2. Social disease is spread by not having sex tonight. (Not necessarily.)

3. You cannot have sex tonight at any age. (True, but less frequently.)

4. Not having sex tonight can be injurious to your health. (We suggest moderation in everything.)

5. Is not having sex tonight more prevalent among men than among women? (50/50.)

6. Can one not have sex tonight alone? (Yes, but it requires more willpower.)

7. Is not having sex in the afternoon more popular than not having sex tonight? (Some people prefer not having sex in the morning.)

8. What is the best time not to have sex? (To each his own time.)

9. Are there any mechanical aids useful to not having sex tonight? (Yes. Have you tried chastity suspenders?)

10. Is it better not to have sex tonight clothed or unclothed? (That is a matter of personal preference.)

THE POTENT QUESTION-NAIRE

YOUR PERSONAL REASONS FOR NOT HAVING SEX

1. ______________________________

2. ______________________________

3. ______________________________

4. ______________________________

5. ______________________________

6. ______________________________

7. ______________________________

8. ______________________________

9. ______________________________

10. ______________________________

YOUR FAVORITE **PLACES** FOR NOT HAVING SEX

1. ______________________________

2. ______________________________

3. ______________________________

4. ______________________________

5. ______________________________

6. ______________________________

7. ______________________________

8. ______________________________

9. ______________________________

10. ______________________________

YOUR FAVORITE **MOVIES** TO WATCH WHILE NOT HAVING SEX

1. ____________________

2. ____________________

3. ____________________

4. ____________________

5. ____________________

6. ____________________

7. ____________________

8. ____________________

9. ____________________

10. ____________________

YOUR FAVORITE **FOODS** TO EAT BEFORE NOT HAVING SEX

1. ______________________________

2. ______________________________

3. ______________________________

4. ______________________________

5. ______________________________

6. ______________________________

7. ______________________________

8. ______________________________

9. ______________________________

10. ______________________________

YOUR FAVORITE **BEVERAGES** TO DRINK WHILE NOT HAVING SEX

1. ______________________________

2. ______________________________

3. ______________________________

4. ______________________________

5. ______________________________

6. ______________________________

7. ______________________________

8. ______________________________

9. ______________________________

10. ______________________________

YOUR FAVORITE **MUSIC** TO LISTEN TO WHILE NOT HAVING SEX

1. ______________________________

2. ______________________________

3. ______________________________

4. ______________________________

5. ______________________________

6. ______________________________

7. ______________________________

8. ______________________________

9. ______________________________

10. ______________________________

YOUR FAVORITE **CLOTHES** TO WEAR WHILE NOT HAVING SEX

1. ______________________________

2. ______________________________

3. ______________________________

4. ______________________________

5. ______________________________

6. ______________________________

7. ______________________________

8. ______________________________

9. ______________________________

10. ______________________________

A NOTE FROM DR. POTENT

Dear Reader:

Always keep this book on your bedside table to inspire you in moments of weakness. Travel with it. Refer to it constantly. This book will change your life for the better.

Get out of bed and live!

I. M. Potent M.D